J B Drew
Garstecki, Julia,
Charles Drew : distinguished surgeon
and blood researcher /
$32.79

WITHDRAWN

CHARLES DREW

Distinguished Surgeon and Blood Researcher

by Julia Garstecki

Content Consultant
Jennifer Rogers
History of Technology and Science
Iowa State University

Core Library

An Imprint of Abdo Publishing
abdopublishing.com

abdopublishing.com

Published by Abdo Publishing, a division of ABDO, PO Box 398166, Minneapolis, Minnesota 55439. Copyright © 2016 by Abdo Consulting Group, Inc. International copyrights reserved in all countries. No part of this book may be reproduced in any form without written permission from the publisher. Core Library™ is a trademark and logo of Abdo Publishing.

Printed in the United States of America, North Mankato, Minnesota
032015
092015

Cover Photo: AP Images
Interior Photos: AP Images, 1, 27; Everett Collection/Newscom, 4; John Vachon/US Farm Security Administration, 7; Library of Congress, 10; National Archives and Records Administration, 12; Shutterstock Images, 16; Carol M. Highsmith/Library of Congress, 18; Alfred Eisenstaedt/The LIFE Picture Collection/Getty Images, 22; Shutterstock Images, 28; Keystone/Getty Images, 29; Bettmann/Corbis, 32, 45; Farm Security Administration/Office of War Information/Library of Congress, 35; Harris and Ewing/National Institutes of Health, 36, 43; Jason Lenhart/Daily News-Record/AP Images, 38

Editor: Jenna Gleisner
Series Designer: Becky Daum

Library of Congress Control Number: 2015931129

Cataloging-in-Publication Data
Garstecki, Julia.
 Charles Drew: Distinguished surgeon and blood researcher / Julia Garstecki.
  p. cm. -- (Great minds of science)
Includes bibliographical references and index.
ISBN 978-1-62403-873-0
1. Drew, Charles, 1904-1950--Juvenile literature. 2. Surgeons--United States--Biography--Juvenile literature. 3. African American surgeons--Biography--Juvenile literature. 4. Blood banks--United States--Juvenile literature. I. Title.
617/.092--dc23
[B]   2015931129

CONTENTS

CHAPTER ONE

GROWING UP AFRICAN-AMERICAN

Science and technology were changing lives in the early 1900s. Cars made travel more convenient. Electricity in homes improved daily living. Medical breakthroughs, such as aspirin and vaccines, helped treat and prevent sickness. Charles Drew would also contribute to science. Charles was born in Washington, DC, on June 3, 1904. He lived a short but successful life.

Charles Drew would grow up to change the medical field with his scientific discoveries about blood.

He revolutionized what we know about blood. His scientific discoveries went on to save millions of lives.

Richard and Nora Drew had five children. Charles was the oldest. As an African-American family in the early 1900s, the Drews faced hardships. Schools and housing were segregated. In most places in the United States at the time, this meant African-American families had limited access to schooling. Charles and his family were an exception. Washington, DC, had a large population of African Americans. There were many good schools for African Americans to attend in the area.

Well into the 1900s, many public facilities across the United States were segregated.

The Drew children had access to excellent schools, but Charles focused more on sports. He was an award-winning athlete at Dunbar High School. He was an excellent swimmer and also participated in football, basketball, baseball, and track.

An Interest in Medicine

When Charles was 16, influenza, or the flu, spread across the United States. The illness was so severe that all gathering places, including schools, were closed. Treatment centers were available for only white people. Charles's sister Elsie died from the illness in 1920. It was Charles's first experience with a serious illness.

Two years later Drew graduated from Dunbar High School. He was awarded an athletic scholarship to Amherst College in Massachusetts. He became a legend on the football and track

The Influenza Pandemic of 1918

The Influenza Pandemic of 1918 began as World War I (1914–1918) ended. A pandemic is a disease or illness that spreads across the world. Soldiers from many countries were fighting in Europe. Some became sick while fighting. When US soldiers came home, many brought the illness with them. An estimated 20 to 40 million people around the world died from influenza during the pandemic. In the United States, approximately 675,000 people died from the illness.

teams at Amherst. Drew was once injured during a football game. He had to be hospitalized. This experience, along with the memory of his sister's illness, influenced Drew to study medicine. After graduating from Amherst College in 1926, he applied to medical school.

Teaching Biology and Chemistry

To earn money for medical school, Drew became a biology and chemistry teacher at Morgan College in Baltimore, Maryland. As usual Drew was better known for his athletic ability. In his short time teaching at the college, he became the athletic director. He also worked to improve its sports program. While applying to medical school, Drew realized he had few options. Most medical schools did not admit African Americans. Harvard accepted only a few nonwhite students each year. Harvard accepted Drew into their program. But he would have to wait until the following fall to attend.

Drew was also involved with sports at Amherst College in Massachusetts.

Drew was anxious to get started. He learned that McGill University in Montreal, Canada, had an excellent medical school. McGill was also known for good treatment of minorities. Also appealing to Drew was that graduate students were allowed to play on the school's sports teams. Drew was accepted in 1928.

At McGill he was able to continue his athletic career while attending classes. This time, Drew was both a star on the field and in the classroom. It wouldn't be long until Drew discovered his life's passion: working with and learning more about blood to help others.

EXPLORE ONLINE

In Chapter One you read about Charles Drew and his love of sports. In the early 1900s, African Americans were fighting for many rights, including the right to play professional sports. Visit the website below to learn about Charles W. Follis, the first African-American professional football player. What hardships did both Charles Drew and Charles W. Follis face as African Americans? How were their lives different? How were their lives the same?

Paving the Way
mycorelibrary.com/charles-drew

CHAPTER TWO

BECOMING DR. CHARLES DREW

Drew was an excellent student at McGill. He did best in anatomy and physiology. He also studied pathology, or the science of diseases, and internal medicine. To become a doctor and surgeon, Drew needed to gain experience. He would do this by working alongside expert doctors and treating patients through an internship.

Drew rose above racial discrimination and worked hard to become a doctor and surgeon.

Learning about Blood Transfusions

During his internship at Montreal General Hospital, Drew met Dr. John Beattie in 1930. Dr. Beattie was a visiting surgeon from England. Drew became interested in blood transfusions after working with Dr. Beattie. Blood transfusions replace blood that is lost during surgery or due to serious injury or illness. During a transfusion, donated blood is added to the patient's blood. Dr. Beattie learned that restoring blood volume with a transfusion was the best way to treat patients suffering from shock.

Blood Types and Transfusions

In 1901 scientist Karl Landsteiner determined there were different blood types: A, B, and O. Later AB was discovered. This was a major breakthrough in blood research. This was important to Dr. Beattie and his work with blood transfusions. Mixing different blood types during transfusions can make blood clump together, or clot, and possibly cause death. The discovery of different blood types made transfusions safer. Charles Drew would need this information when he began studying blood transfusions while at McGill.

Shock can occur when the body loses too much blood. But at this time, there was no way to store blood for long periods of time. Donors had to be close to the patients they were giving blood to. Many people died because blood was not available when they needed it.

Drew Gets an Idea

During Drew's internship, there was a fire at the Montreal General Hospital. Many patients were badly burned and went into shock. Drew treated as many patients as he could, but there was not enough blood for all of them. He also witnessed bleeding patients die when matching blood could not be found. Drew recognized the need for a reliable blood supply. He graduated from McGill and went on to earn his medical degree and master of surgery degree in 1933. He was now a doctor and surgeon. Drew still wanted to learn more. He hoped to train at the Mayo Clinic, a prestigious hospital in Minnesota. Mayo Clinic would not accept Drew because of his race. Drew was

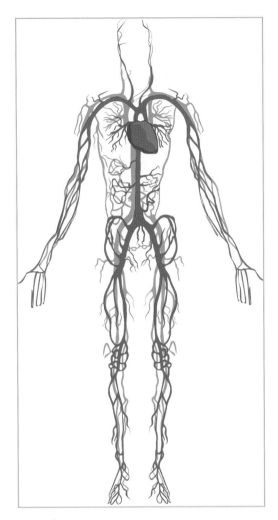

The Circulatory System

Look at this diagram of the body's circulatory system. Arteries are shown in red. These vessels carry blood from the heart to other parts of the body. Veins are shown in blue. They carry blood back to the heart, where it is pumped through again, always circulating. Notice all of the different arteries and veins carrying blood through the body. How does seeing this diagram better help you visualize blood circulation and how blood transfusions are especially important in times of shock or other medical emergencies? How does this diagram better help you understand the importance of Drew's concern and work with blood?

discovering white patients wanted only white doctors to treat them.

A Different Path

Instead of going to Mayo Clinic, Drew applied for a teaching job at Howard University in Washington, DC, where African Americans were accepted. He was hired to teach pathology.

It was a fortunate time to be hired at Howard University. The school had received money from the Rockefeller Foundation's General Education Board. This organization supported education opportunities for African Americans. The board gave the school money to train teachers and administrators. Some of the money funded a five-year training program for four African-American teachers. These teachers would learn from the best doctors and surgeons. At the end of their training, they would lead the Howard University Medical School. Drew was chosen as one of the four teachers. He was selected to study clinical surgery.

At Howard University, Drew taught students to recognize different diseases and discover what caused them.

Drew Gets Recognized

Howard University hired expert surgeon Edward Lee Howes in 1936 to teach African-American students, including Drew. Drew worked with Dr. Howes, assisting in surgeries from 1936 until 1938. Drew was recognized for his intelligence and hard work and was invited to study at Columbia University's medical school for two years. The Rockefeller Foundation would pay for it. Then he would come back to Howard University to teach others what he learned.

Experiments with Blood

In 1939 Drew worked with Dr. John Scudder at Columbia University. Together, along with other doctors, they studied blood storage. The team collected blood samples and placed them in different tubes. Then they added carbon dioxide to some of the tubes to see what would happen. They discovered that blood mixed with the carbon dioxide did not clot and

Earning Respect

Allen O. Whipple was in charge of the medical program at Columbia University. His students took classes at Columbia and then interned at Presbyterian Hospital in New York City. No African American had ever worked in a Presbyterian Hospital before. Other students and doctors assumed Drew would stay in the laboratory and process information. They did not think he would see patients. Drew worked hard and had a positive attitude. He was determined to see patients. With time he earned the respect of Dr. Whipple.

separate. This would lengthen how long the blood could last outside of the human body. This information would help lengthen the period of time blood could be used for transfusions. Drew also learned that if he separated the blood into different components and refrigerated them separately, the components lasted longer than whole blood did. The information Drew was learning would soon result in his first major contribution to society: the blood bank.

US Army Captain Oswald H. Robertson wrote the following journal entry during World War I (1914–1918) on November 30, 1917. This journal entry explains the importance of discovering new methods for blood transfusions, especially in emergency situations:

> The beds were filled and we began putting stretchers on the floor . . . blood everywhere—clothes soaked in the blood, pools of blood in the stretchers, streams of blood dropping from the stretchers to the floor.
>
> . . .
>
> They were dying faster than we could get them out . . . I could transfuse an occasional one but the majority had to take their chance without much treatment and go [through] operation as best they could provided there was any possibility at all of their standing operation . . .

> Source: Lynn G. Stansbury and John R. Hess. "Blood Transfusion in World War I: The Roles of Lawrence Bruce Robertson and Oswald Hope Robertson in the 'Most Important Medical Advance of the War.'" PubMed.gov. National Center for Biotechnology Information, n.d. Web. Accessed February 10, 2015.

Back It Up

The author of this passage is using evidence to support a point. Write a paragraph describing the point the author is making. Then write down two or three pieces of evidence the author uses to make the point.

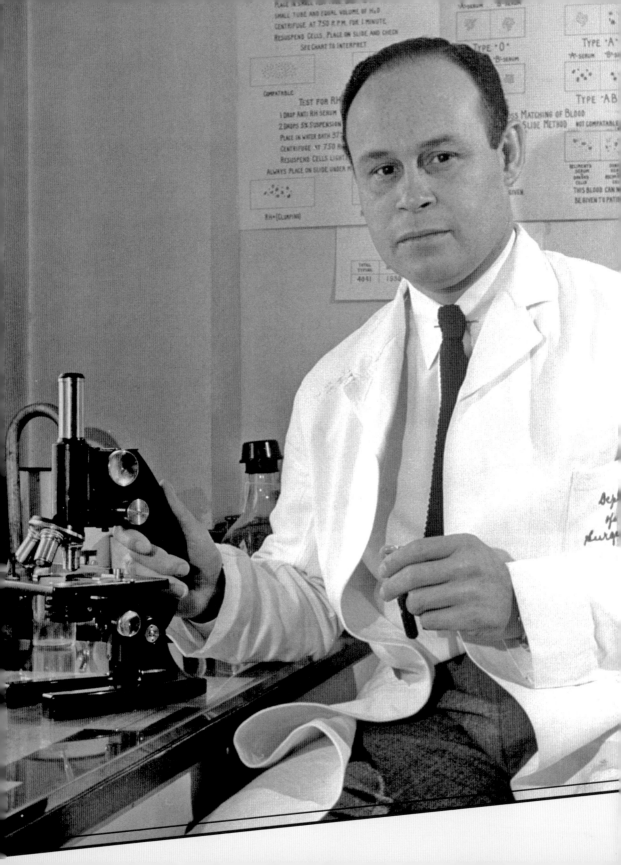

CREATING A BLOOD BANK

Drew wanted to figure out how best to store blood. This would make blood better available when it was needed. Blood starts to clot and break down when it is stored. While at Columbia, Drew gathered all of the information he could about transfusions, including its history and all current research. He learned what had been tested and why some experiments worked. He

Drew was determined to find a way to bank blood.

evaluated everything he found and shared his findings with other experts. Once Drew was finished with his research, he had written the most complete paper ever printed on the topic of stored blood. It was titled "Banked Blood: A Study in Blood Preservation." Experts on the topic called the paper a masterpiece.

A Life-Saving Experiment

As Drew researched information for his paper, Columbia gave him and Dr. Scudder money to try a new experiment. It would be the first attempt to create a blood bank. The goal was to be able to bank, or store, large amounts of blood in case of emergency. If it worked, hospitals all around the world would be able to set up blood banks. Drew studied all of the things that might affect blood. He even experimented with the way blood was stored. Did the shape of the containers make a difference? How should it be collected? At what temperature should it be stored? Drew was determined to answer these questions with his experiments.

Drew's experiment lasted seven months. Because of his work, he earned his doctor of medical science degree in 1940. Then his two years at Columbia were finished, and Drew returned to Howard University. He was an assistant professor of surgery and a surgeon back at Freedmen's Hospital.

An Unexpected Turn of Events

Drew hoped to create a team of expert surgeons at Howard University. But that goal would have to wait. The United

Banking Steps

Many steps were involved in Drew's blood banking experiments. Blood had to be collected with sterile, or clean, equipment. It also had to be placed in sterile containers. This would keep germs from contaminating the blood. After collection, the blood had to be treated so that it would not clot. It also had to be refrigerated at a certain temperature. Donors had to be found, scheduled, and screened for health problems. The blood had to be tested for diseases. Nurses and laboratory workers needed to be trained to collect, handle, and test the blood. Procedures needed to be written, followed, and recorded.

States was quickly becoming involved in World War II (1939–1945). In June 1940, the New York Academy of Medicine brought together experts in blood research, including Drew and Dr. Scudder. The academy wanted to collect and ship blood to the Allied troops—those the United States supported—in Europe. This would be called the Blood for Britain project.

The Importance of Plasma

Instead of sending blood, Dr. Scudder suggested they send plasma. Plasma is the liquid part of blood. It is made up of water and has many functions, including maintaining blood pressure and volume. It is important because it is responsible for making sure cells function as they should in the body. Many doctors, including Dr. Scudder and Dr. Drew, had experimented with plasma for transfusions. Plasma can be separated from blood cells. The plasma can then be used to replace fluids and treat shock. It lasts longer than blood and doesn't break down when it is moved from place to place. It can be frozen quickly

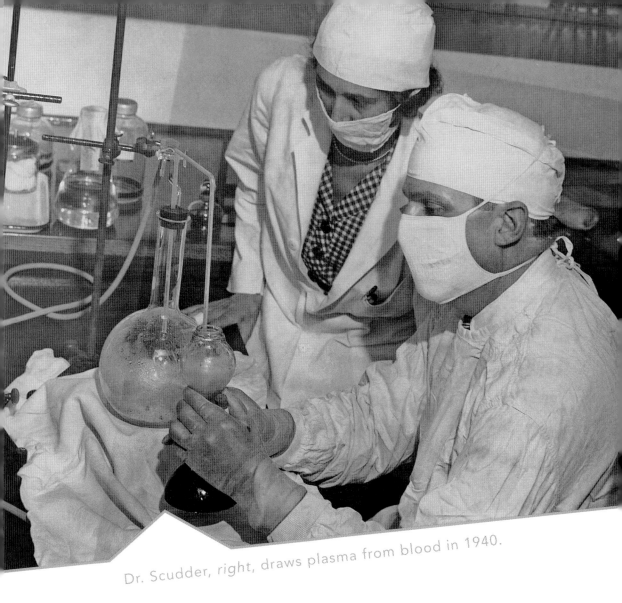

Dr. Scudder, right, draws plasma from blood in 1940.

and stored up to a year, then thawed right before it is needed. It can also be used with any blood type, and it is less likely to carry diseases.

Drew and Dr. Scudder knew they would have to collect a greater amount of blood than they had in

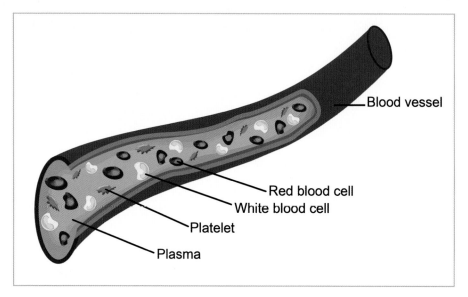

Blood vessel

Red blood cell

White blood cell

Platelet

Plasma

Blood Composition

Drew and his colleagues studied ways to bring life-saving blood to soldiers on the battlefields. Through research, they discovered there were many parts to blood. This diagram shows the different parts of blood. What is the primary component? How does seeing this diagram better help you understand Drew's work with blood plasma?

previous experiments. This time they would have to collect, organize, and store large amounts of plasma from many different hospitals. They also had to set up procedures to remove the plasma from the blood and keep it healthy for its journey to Britain, where soldiers could receive it.

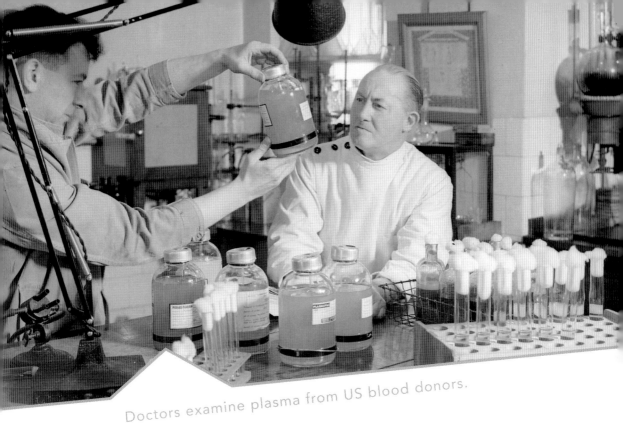

Doctors examine plasma from US blood donors.

Blood for Britain Project

Drew was chosen to be the full-time medical supervisor on the Blood for Britain project in the fall of 1940. The Red Cross, an organization that helps people in need all around the world, called for volunteer blood donors. Newspapers, radio commercials, and posters advertised for donors. Six hospitals in the New York City area were prepared for appointments. Blood donations began August 15, 1940.

Many people were involved in the Blood for Britain project. People in the United States donated blood. Then doctors and nurses removed the plasma, packaged it, and shipped it to England. Once in England, doctors and nurses examined the plasma to make sure it was still healthy. It was then given to wounded soldiers who needed it.

Many doctors assisted with the project, but Drew is credited with the project's success. He had gathered the information and determined how to collect and store large amounts of blood and plasma for use in emergency situations.

Contaminated Plasma

One of the biggest challenges during the Blood for Britain project was contamination. Plasma was collected at several different hospitals in the United States. Keeping all of the equipment clean during the collection, storage, and shipment of plasma was difficult. Some reports suggest the project stopped after much of the plasma was found contaminated, and therefore not useable, when it reached Britain in January 1941.

Lessons Learned

The Blood for Britain team learned a lot during the program. Dried plasma worked better for storage and transport. But more research was needed to make the use of dried plasma possible. The biggest lesson Drew and his men learned was that blood must be completely sealed to remain sterile and useable. In February 1941, it looked as if the United States would be entering the war. Now Drew was needed to help US soldiers.

FURTHER EVIDENCE

Chapter Three discusses Charles Drew's life as a blood researcher. What main idea or ideas does the chapter share about his journey to learn more about blood? Read more about Drew at the website below. Find a quote about his work. Does the quote support the ideas in this chapter, or does it add new information?

Charles Drew Biography
mycorelibrary.com/charles-drew

CHAPTER FOUR

DREW AND THE RED CROSS

Drew was a well-known expert on the topic of blood. Red Cross officials who worked with him on the Blood for Britain project respected him. They asked him to become the medical director of the first American Red Cross Blood Bank in New York in 1941. Blood collected would be used to help US Army and Navy soldiers in

Drew's work with banking blood helped bring blood to troops during World War II.

need. If the program in New York was successful, it would expand throughout the country.

Like the Blood for Britain project, many doctors are credited with the development of blood banking. But Drew is recognized as creating the first blood donor service. To increase blood donations, Drew created a mobile blood collection unit. Today these are known as bloodmobiles. Large trucks were loaded with supplies for collecting and storing blood and keeping it cool. Many churches and schools served as donation centers.

The Red Cross

The Red Cross helps lessen human suffering around the world. There are many ways the Red Cross helps people. When disaster strikes, such as floods or fires, the Red Cross provides emergency care. This includes providing safe drinking water and warm blankets to those in need. The Red Cross also provides health education, such as teaching disaster preparedness skills or CPR training. More than 40 percent of America's donated blood supply is collected and distributed by the Red Cross.

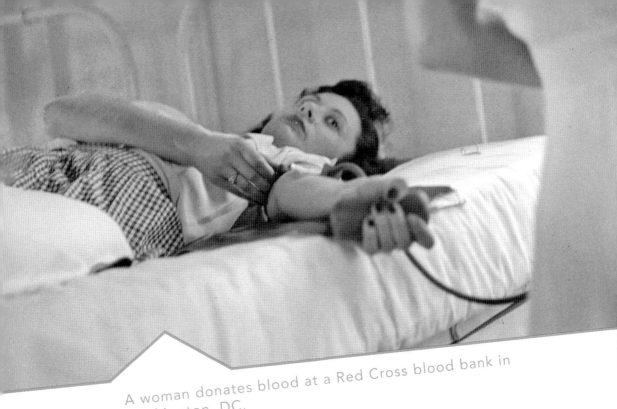

A woman donates blood at a Red Cross blood bank in Washington, DC.

Dr. Drew Leaves the Red Cross

Unfortunately Drew would not keep his job as medical director for long. Drew clearly saved the lives of many, but racism was still a problem in the United States in the 1930s and 1940s. Blood donations were segregated. The military stated that donor blood should be sorted by race. It also said that African-American donors should be rejected. Drew quit his position at the Red Cross. He argued that race did not affect blood. Other experts in blood research

At Howard University, Drew taught his students that they could overcome boundaries if they excelled in their work.

said the same. In 1942 the Red Cross allowed African Americans to donate blood. But African-American blood was still kept separate.

Back to Teaching

Drew returned to Howard University in April 1941. Between 1941 and 1950, he taught many African-American students. He was a passionate teacher. African Americans rarely received the same medical care as white people did. Drew was convinced that creating more African-American doctors would help fix that issue.

In 1942 Drew became the first African-American examiner for the American Board of Surgery. He was the chief of staff at

Charles R. Drew University

Drew made numerous contributions to medicine, and he helped break barriers for minorities. Many people he worked with did not believe African Americans should be able to treat white patients. When Drew returned to Howard University, he was committed to teaching African Americans so they could better serve their communities. His passion continues today at Charles R. Drew University in Los Angeles, California. Medical students at this university are trained specifically to treat underserved communities. Most students attending are minorities, similar to the students Drew taught.

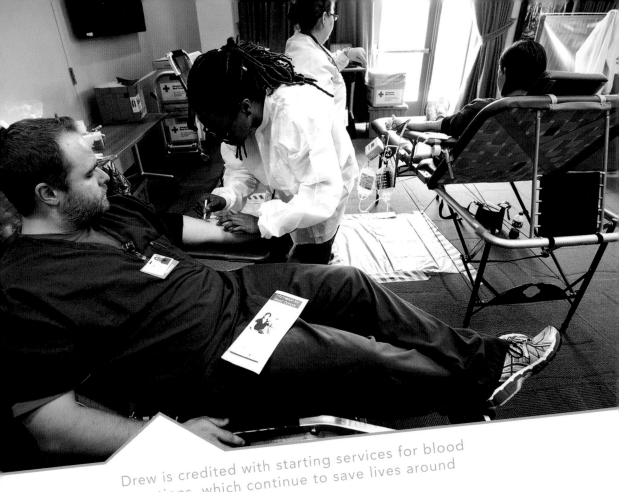

Drew is credited with starting services for blood donations, which continue to save lives around the world.

Freedmen's Hospital in Washington, DC, from 1944 to 1946 and was the medical director of Freedmen's Hospital for two years after that. In 1944 the National Association for the Advancement of Colored People (NAACP) honored Drew. The NAACP is a civil rights organization. It works to promote equal rights for all people. The NAACP awarded Drew with the Spingarn

Medal for his achievements with blood plasma and distribution. Drew continued his work as chief surgeon at Freedmen's Hospital and as a professor at Howard University until 1950.

The Death of Dr. Drew

Every year free medical clinics were held in Tuskegee, Alabama. Drew looked forward to the annual event. He enjoyed working with other doctors and inspiring African-American medical students. In 1950, while driving through North Carolina to Tuskegee with three other doctors, Drew fell asleep at the wheel and crashed his car.

Drew was brought to Alamance General Hospital. Some people wonder if Drew received adequate medical care. Hospitals were still segregated, and African Americans did not always receive the best care. But the doctors who were with Drew at the time insist everything was done to try to save him. Unfortunately Drew's injuries were too severe. He died at the age of 45.

It is uncertain what more Charles Drew could have accomplished had he not died so young. Yet he is considered one of the most accomplished surgeons of his time. His research about blood transfusions saved thousands of lives. And his methods for banking blood are still used by the American Red Cross and hospitals around the world. In addition to his accomplishments in the medical field, Drew strived to give more opportunities to minorities, especially in the medical field in the United States.

Drew was very upset to learn the Army would not take blood from African Americans. Drew wrote a letter on April 15, 1944, to Army official Jacob Billikopf, expressing his disagreement:

> Dear Mr. Billikopf:
>
> . . . .
>
> I think that the Army made a grievous mistake, a stupid error in first issuing an order to the effect that blood for the Army should not be received from Negroes. It was a bad mistake for three reasons: (1) No official department of the Federal Government should willfully humiliate its citizens; (2) There is no scientific basis for the order; (3) They need the blood. I would be heartily in favor of pressure of all types being brought on the Surgeon General of the U.S. Army to force him to rescind the instructions to the American Red Cross which demands the separation of the bloods of the donors.

Source: "Letter from Charles R. Drew to Jacob Billikopf." The Charles R. Drew Papers. US National Library of Medicine, n.d. Web. Accessed February 12, 2015.

What's the Big Idea?

Take a close look at this editorial. What is the author trying to say? Pick out two details the author uses to make a point. Does he agree or disagree with Billikopf's actions? What is the tone of Dr. Drew's letter? What is its main purpose?

Teaching Future Surgeons

Because of Dr. Charles Drew, many African-American students went on to become expert surgeons. He believed shaping excellent surgeons would be his greatest contribution to the medical field. Dr. Drew had high standards and demanded his students work hard. Dr. Drew knew his well-trained students would help people understand that race was not a factor in what jobs a person could have.

Storing Blood

Because of Charles Drew, many soldiers injured on battlefields were able to survive. Dr. Drew's research helped doctors learn to keep blood in sterile, closed containers. This kept the blood healthy and secure for transport. Doctors today still credit Charles Drew for the advances made in blood research. Drew's discoveries formed the building blocks for how we preserve blood today.

Blood Banks

Dr. Drew organized the first national blood bank. While other doctors stored blood in small amounts, Dr. Drew helped the Red Cross organize an entire system of collecting, storing, and distributing blood. The Red Cross still uses the system that Dr. Drew began decades ago.

Say What?

Learning about medical treatments can mean learning a lot of new vocabulary. Find five words in this book that you have never seen or heard before. Use a dictionary to find out what they mean. Rewrite the meanings in your own words. Then use each word in a new sentence.

Tell the Tale

Chapter Three discusses Drew's research about banking blood. Write 200 words that tell the story of his experiments. Describe the kind of work he performed and what he discovered. Be sure to set the scene, develop a sequence of events, and write a conclusion.

Surprise Me

This book includes a lot of information about blood and the way we use it. After reading this book, what two or three facts about blood did you find most surprising? Write a few sentences about each fact and explain why you found them surprising.

Why Do I Care?

Thinking about blood and blood research can raise many questions. Why is it important for doctors and scientists to know how blood works and can be stored and transfused? What has this knowledge helped us understand and accomplish? Use your imagination and explain your answers.

GLOSSARY

anatomy
the study of the human body

internal medicine
treatment of diseases that do not require surgery

internship
a temporary position with an emphasis on on-the-job training

laboratory
a room or building equipped for scientific experiments, research, or teaching, or for manufacturing drugs or chemicals

pathology
the science of the causes and effects of diseases

physiology
a science that deals with the ways the human body functions

reliable
consistently good in quality; able to be trusted

segregated
set apart or divided along racial, sexual, or religious lines

shock
a medical emergency in which the organs and tissues of the body are not receiving an adequate flow of blood, which can be life-threatening

LEARN MORE

Books

Marsico, Katie. *The Red Cross.* Ann Arbor, MI: Cherry Lake, 2015.

Morrison, Heather S. *Inventors of Health and Medical Technology.* New York: Cavendish, 2016.

Nagelhout, Ryan. *The Heart and Blood in Your Body.* New York: Britannica, 2015.

Websites

To learn more about Great Minds of Science, visit **booklinks.abdopublishing.com.** These links are routinely monitored and updated to provide the most current information available.

Visit **mycorelibrary.com** for free additional tools for teachers and students.

INDEX

ABOUT THE AUTHOR

Julia Garstecki lives in New York with her husband and two children. She studied biology in college and found the study of blood and cells very interesting. While she did not become a doctor, she enjoys writing about medical discoveries.